KT-438-608

THE FORMER PORTUGUESE COLONIES

THE FORMER PORTUGUESE COLONIES

ANGOLA, MOZAMBIQUE, GUINEA–BISSAU, CAPE VERDE, SÃO TOMÉ, AND PRINCIPE

BY HERB BOYD

FRANKLIN WATTS

New York | London | Toronto | Sydney | 1981

A FIRST BOOK

(E.)

S123696

966.

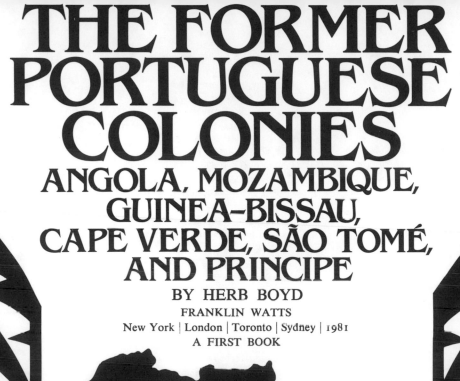

Cover design by Jackie Schuman

Photographs courtesy of:
Wide World: pp. 10, 14;
Sygma (Patrick Chauvel): p. 17;
Sygma (Dix): p. 46;
Rapho/Photo Researchers, Inc.
(J. Allan Cash): p. 22;
United Nations/Ciric-Geneva: p. 25;
United Nations/Van Lierop: p. 32;
United Press International: p. 35;
TASS from Sovfoto:
pp. 41 (G. Alexeyev), 50 (L. Vorontsov);
Amica/Gamma Liaison Agency, Inc.: p. 49.

Maps courtesy of Vantage Art.

Library of Congress Cataloging in Publication Data

Boyd, Herb, 1938–
The former Portuguese colonies.

(A First book)
Bibliography: p.
Includes index.
SUMMARY: Background and up-to-date facts and figures
about six African countries.
1. Portugal—Colonies—Africa—Juvenile literature.
2. Africa—Juvenile literature. [1. Africa.
2. Portugal—Colonies—Africa] I. Title.
DT36.B69   966   80–24752
ISBN 0–531–04273–1

Copyright © 1981 by Herb Boyd
All rights reserved
Printed in the United States of America
6   5   4   3   2   1

To my children—
Almitra, Katherine, Johnny, and Maya.
And to the memory of
Walter Rodney.

CONTENTS

THE FORMER PORTUGUESE COLONIES

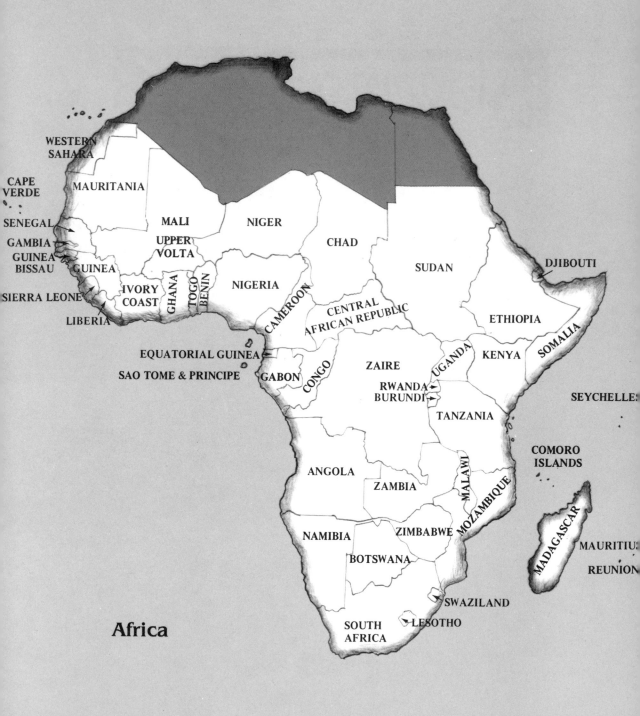

WESTERN
SAHARA

CAPE
VERDE

MAURITANIA

SENEGAL

GAMBIA

GUINEA
BISSAU

GUINEA

SIERRA LEONE

LIBERIA

MALI

UPPER
VOLTA

IVORY
COAST

GHANA

TOGO

BENIN

NIGER

NIGERIA

CAMEROON

CHAD

CENTRAL
AFRICAN REPUBLIC

SUDAN

DJIBOUTI

ETHIOPIA

SOMALIA

EQUATORIAL GUINEA

SAO TOME & PRINCIPE

GABON

CONGO

ZAIRE

RWANDA
BURUNDI

UGANDA

KENYA

SEYCHELLES

TANZANIA

COMORO
ISLANDS

ANGOLA

ZAMBIA

MALAWI

MOZAMBIQUE

MADAGASCAR

MAURITIUS

REUNION

NAMIBIA

ZIMBABWE

BOTSWANA

SWAZILAND

LESOTHO

SOUTH
AFRICA

Africa

1
PORTUGAL IN AFRICA—500 YEARS OF COLONIALISM

Africa's contact with Europe goes back thousands of years. Long before written history, Europeans and the people living in and around the Mediterranean had begun to wander into Egypt and to roam across the countries of North Africa. Only the vast expanses of the Sahara desert delayed Europe's penetration into the southern portion of the African continent.

But the desert could not remain a barrier forever, and by the early fifteenth century (1400s) Western European powers, mainly the Portuguese and the Spanish, began their sea explorations beyond the Strait of Gibraltar and along the coast of West Africa.

The Portuguese sailors and merchants, under the supervision of Prince Henry the Navigator, led the way, and before the end of the century they had established trade relations with the native population. At first, the Portuguese traders were only interested in basic African commodities—nuts, palm oil, fruit, ivory, spices, and gold—but as explorations increased in the Americas, and there arose a need for laborers to work the land, the Portuguese began to demand more and more slaves—Africa's black gold.

This was the beginning of the brutal Atlantic slave trade, and it is estimated that between 1450 and 1500 more than 150,000 African slaves were taken by the Portuguese in West Africa. In the succeeding years this number would escalate into the millions as the Portuguese fought with the Dutch, the French, and the English for the monopoly of this trade in human souls.

After four hundred years of trafficking in slaves, with Angola alone suffering the loss of more than three million people to the trade, the Portuguese government, in 1836, put an end to the vicious practice. However, it was not to be completely abolished until well into the twentieth century.

During the centuries of the slave trade, the Portuguese empire had extended from one end of the world to the other. With the riches gained from slaving, there were also large profits from the plantations of Brazil and from trade in spices from South Asia. Settlements, trading posts, and major forts were established to oversee Portuguese operations in Bahia, Elmina, Goa, São Tomé, Mombasa, and Sofala. The basic elements of Portuguese colonialism and control in Africa, although still shaky in some regions, were now falling into place. To secure its dominion, only one more action was needed.

And that came in 1884–85 at the Berlin Conference, when Portugal and the other European powers met and signed the Berlin Treaty. This treaty set forth the rules and guidelines by which the European nations could conquer and divide Africa among themselves. The "scramble for Africa" was now given official sanction.

Portugal, having already seized vast stretches of African territory, welcomed a treaty that approved colonial occupation and, at the same time, checked the aggressive aims of Germany and Great Britain.

From the signing of the Berlin Treaty until World War I, Portugal's involvement in Africa was a story of attempted conquest and bitter conflict. After the closing of the lucrative slave trade, Portugal's economic and political power declined considerably.

Portugal's diminishing fortunes continued into the 1930s, and its conservative colonial policy became even more rigid when the longtime dictator, Prime Minister Antonio de Oliveira Salazar, took control of the government in 1932. One of the primary aims of Salazar's administration was to continue Portugal's Christian mission of "civilizing the backward people" of Africa.

After World War II, with other European powers releasing their hold on colonial empires, Portugal stubbornly held on to its possessions. Unlike the economies of Great Britain and France, Portugal's economic well-being was directly tied to its colonies. To grant independence to Angola or to Mozambique would have been disastrous for a country clearly the poorest and the least developed in Western Europe.

The rise of African nationalism that swept across the continent in the early part of the twentieth century did not occur in Portugal's "overseas provinces," or colonies, until the 1960s. The first sign of armed struggle from freedom fighters occurred in Angola, and the winds of change blew these revolutionary sparks from one colony to another. Independence was on the way. This is the story that will unfold as we discuss the separate histories of these former Portuguese colonies.

[3]

2

ANGOLA

Of all the former Portuguese colonies, Angola was considered to be the jewel. Scattered over its vast territory was an abundant supply of valuable resources—ivory, spices, various minerals (including the later-to-be discovered oil and diamonds), and slaves. But to gather this potential wealth the early Portuguese explorers and traders had to overcome many challenges and hardships.

Not only were there inland climatic conditions and tropical diseases to conquer, but there also loomed before them a formidable resistance from the Africans. It was well into the twentieth century before Portuguese domination was fully extended across Angola. However, this domination would be short-lived and costly and would give the Africans both a common enemy and a new sense of unity.

Nationalism was the next development, and as it would be in the other "overseas provinces" of Portugal, revolution was the

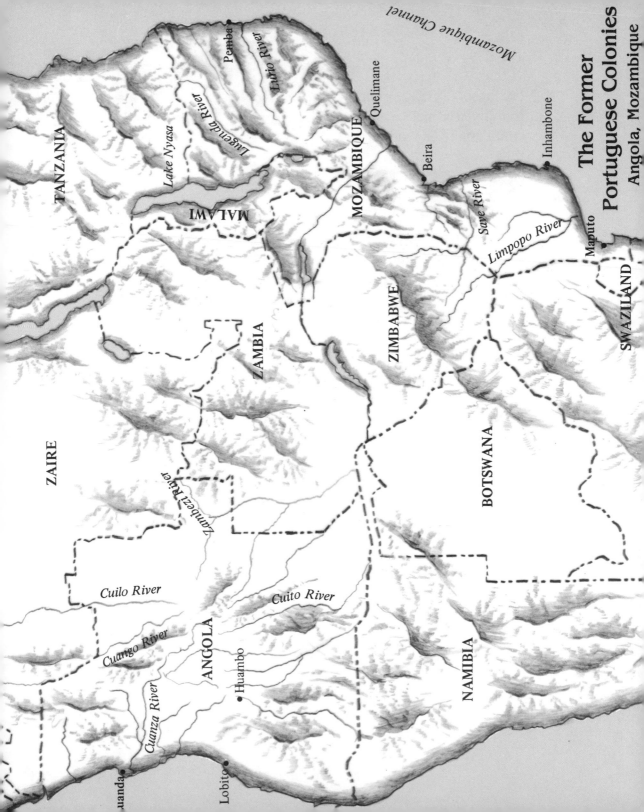

The Former
Portuguese Colonies
Angola, Mozambique

Mozambique Channel

TANZANIA

Pemba

Lurio River

Lugenda River

Lake Nyasa

MALAWI

Quelimane

MOZAMBIQUE

Beira

Inhambone

Save River

Limpopo River

Maputo

SWAZILAND

ZAMBIA

ZIMBABWE

ZAIRE

BOTSWANA

Zambezi River

Cuilo River

Cuito River

NAMIBIA

Cuango River

ANGOLA

Huambo

Cuanza River

Luanda

Lobito

end result. Unfortunately, Angola would have to endure a brutally destructive civil war before peace and independence could finally be secured.

GEOGRAPHY, CLIMATE, AND POPULATION

With its area of 478,350 square miles (1,237,926 sq km), Angola is among the larger countries of Africa. It is fourteen times larger than Portugal. Like Mozambique, Angola has an extensive coastline (1,000 miles/1,600 km). Beyond this narrow coastal strip there is a series of plateaus and tablelands, some of which rise to 7,000 feet (2,134 m).

Angola, almost evenly divided by the east-west Benguela railroad, is bordered on the north and northeast by Zaire (formerly the Republic of the Congo-Kinshasa), on the east by Zambia, and by Namibia (formerly South West Africa) to the south. For the most part, Angola possesses a tropical climate. However, the cold Benguela current gives the southern coastal area a dry, desert-like quality.

From May to September it is generally dry, while the rainy season occurs between October and May. The country also contains a number of river systems, and the Zambezi, which flows through Mozambique, has its headwaters in Angola.

The population of Angola prior to the civil war in 1974 was estimated at five and a half million. Of this estimate, Europeans numbered just over 300,000. Angola's comparatively small population is primarily the result of widespread tribal warfare, often instigated by the colonial invaders throughout the centuries of slave trade. Millions of Africans were forced from their homeland and shipped to the West during the slave trade. And of all the countries in Africa ravaged by the slave trade, the territory of Angola probably lost the greatest number of people.

In recent times, the growth of population has been further hindered by a devastating civil war which left thousands of casualties in its wake.

THE PEOPLE

The tribal structure of Angola is divided into four major ethnic-linguistic groups—Ovimbundu, Mbundu (or Kimbundu), Bakongo (or Kikongo), and Lunda-Chokwe. Of these, the Ovimbundu, who dwell in the central highlands of Angola, number well over two million and are the largest group.

Other ethnic groups include the Nganguela or Ganguela, Nhaneka-Humbe, Kwanyama, and the Ovambo and Herrero, found mostly in Namibia. There are also a small number of non-Bantu speaking people, most notably the Hottentot-Bushmen located in the southern region of the country.

Many of these ethnic divisions, especially the Ovimbundu, Mbundu (a group once ruled by King Ndola from which the name Angola is derived), Bakongo, and Lunda-Chokwe had a direct impact on the development of the major nationalist organizations active today in the country.

More specifically, the FNLA (National Front for the Liberation of Angola) was comprised mainly of Bakongos, a group with strong ethnic ties to the great kingdom of the Congo. For the MPLA (Popular Movement for the Liberation of Angola) the Mbundu were the dominant ethnic group, while the Ovimbundu and the Lunda-Chokwe were the two most significant groups

[7]

within UNITA (National Union for the Total Independence of Angola).

Much of the age-old rivalry existing between the groups was intensified by the Portuguese during the slave trade era. The civil war also sharpened the differences between the various ethnic groups.

In an effort to unify the people of Angola, these ethnic differences are no longer encouraged. However, the simmering remains of the civil war in parts of southern Angola continue to hamper the government's drive toward peace and national unity.

ECONOMY, EDUCATION, AND RELIGION

For centuries, Angola's economy and material wealth were rigidly locked within the Portuguese colonial system: all able-bodied African males were required to work for the colonial administration; old men, women, and children were assigned to traditional agricultural tasks; and the wealth obtained from the country's valuable minerals and natural resources was the exclusive property of the Portuguese.

This policy enriched Portugal and robbed Angola of its priceless resources and consequent growth. Through this colonial practice, technological and industrial development was delayed in Angola. And with the majority of African workers forced to carry out only hard-labor assignments, skilled laborers were rarely available.

The general underdevelopment of Angola was extensive and touched every sector of the society. Perhaps the best example of this lack of development is in the realm of education. Before 1960, only one or two percent of Angola's population was literate. To some degree, it was possible for Africans, particularly the *mestiços,* or people of mixed ancestry, to assimilate into Portuguese life, but the guarantees of formal training and a good education were withheld.

In the 1800s, Christian missionaries were sent from European countries to improve the African's lot through education and religious training. For the most part, however, they not only failed in this mission, but also disrupted the African way of life. Whether Catholic or Protestant, the church demanded a loyalty that drastically undercut the traditional authority maintained through tribal and kinship ties.

Today, great change is currently under way in both religion and education. Even in the rural countryside of Angola, the government's plan to eradicate illiteracy is beginning to take effect. Religious practice is left to the individual, with the majority of Angolans retaining their traditional African beliefs.

Today, agriculture is the basis of the economy. Although coffee, sisal (a hard fiber used in the making of twine), iron ore, sugar, and diamonds are among Angola's chief exports, petroleum from the rich oil fields of Cabinda is fast becoming the major source of revenue on the foreign market. New industry is also being developed in aluminum, and the rich deposits of gold and copper should also improve the country's economic standing.

HISTORY: COLONIALISM
AND RESISTANCE

Certainly, Angola's history does not begin with the coming of the Portuguese. Still, little is known of the country's earlier dynasties and kingdoms. In fact, it was only after Luanda began to show some commercial importance, and Angola was able to de-

feat invading forces from the Congo in 1556, that Angola truly emerged on the world scene.

Shortly after this success, a civil war ensued in the Congo, and the Portuguese gradually shifted their attention from the Congo to Angola. This also meant that the slave trade was passed on to Angola. Despite strong African resistance, by the first decade of the sixteenth century the slave trade was flourishing, and Portugal was strengthening its hold on Angola.

During this period, the great Queen Nzinga or "Jinga" came to power and temporarily brought the various northwest kingdoms of Angola together. The alliance she created did not last very long, and after several campaigns against the Portuguese, Nzinga withdrew her forces and turned her attention to the conquest of Matamba. This was her final major victory, and until her death in 1663, Nzinga maintained close commercial ties with the Portuguese.

From the early 1800s to the 1850s, the Portuguese struggled to hold dominance along the Angolan coast. Included in a series of victories were the defeat of the Dutch, who had defeated them in 1641; the suppression of the Ndongo of northwest Angola; and the pacification of Ngola Kanini, leader of the Matambas who had administered a number of costly setbacks to the Portuguese. Complete control of the northwest did not come until well into the twentieth century, with the defeat of the Dembos.

Toward the south of Angola, in the central highlands, a

Young girls singing hymns at an outdoor Christian service in Luanda, the capital of Angola.

similar story of resistance to Portuguese colonialism had occurred. Foremost among the resisters were the warriors from the Ovimbundu kingdoms. For more than two hundred and fifty years the Ovimbundu waged war with the Portuguese. By 1904, the same year in which the Kwanyama people (located further south) ambushed and killed a battalion of Portuguese soldiers, peace had returned to the kingdom of the Ovimbundu. It would take a few more years before the conflict subsided completely in the kingdoms further south.

FROM NATIONALISM
TO REVOLUTION

African resistance to colonization was as common as it was widespread. From all over Angola, the Portuguese attempts to pacify the colony were met with organized and sustained military resistance. Queen Nzinga, Ngola Kanini, Mutu-ya-Kevela, and Chief Kassela were just four of the leaders whose armies waged battle after battle with the Portuguese over the last several hundred years.

The spirit of struggle and resistance had long been a part of the Angolan experience; therefore, it was hardly surprising that in the 1940s rebellion was again taking shape. The new attitude of militancy and revolt surfaced in the many publications and cultural associations that were springing up all over Angola in the mid-1950s. There were *Liga Angolana,* the Angolan United Front (FUA), the Sociedad Cultural de Angola, the Party of Struggle of Africans of Angola (PLUA), as well as the Angolan Communist Party (PCA).

Important artists and revolutionaries such as Viriato de Cruz, Mario de Andrade, and the late Agostinho Neto, Angola's first president, were among the members who founded these radical organizations. Along with such illustrious patriots as Amilcar Cabral of Guinea-Bissau and Marcelino dos Santos of Mozambique, they shared a common goal—the liberation of their colonies.

It was through the cultural associations and their members that a climate of political unrest was created. To counter this growing dissent, the Portuguese unleashed the dreaded PIDE (Portuguese police). In 1959 and 1960 hundreds of radical and liberal Europeans, mestiço, and African intellectuals were arrested. Similar moves to suppress the possibility of a nationalist uprising were also being carried out in the countryside by the Portuguese army.

But none of these measures were successful, and by February 1961 the attacks on Luanda Central Prison marked the beginning of Angola's national liberation struggle. As the revolution developed in Angola, armed struggle was also launched in Guinea-Bissau (1963) and Mozambique (1964). The 100,000 soldiers from Portugal were now forced to fight in three colonies —and on several fronts within each colony. A decade later, guerilla warfare would still be the predominant activity in the three colonies.

In April 1974 the fascist regime in Portugal received the death blow. A group of young officers, taking their cue from a failing war in the colonies and the hopelessness of victory, overthrew the government of Portugal. In a bold initiative, which has come to be called the "Captain's Coup," this group of Portuguese officers, pledging a policy of decolonization, quickly put an end to a half century of Portuguese fascism.

By November of the same year, delegations from MPLA,

Students in Luanda crossing a street.
Since Angola's independence, great efforts
have been made to build more schools
and better educate the people.

FNLA, and UNITA arrived in Luanda to make firm the cease-fire agreements signed by MPLA and a representative of the Portuguese army. The Portuguese had been thoroughly defeated, but a still bloodier conflict awaited the victorious liberation movements.

THE CIVIL WAR

The civil war in Angola, like most civil wars, was a mutually destructive affair that even now, with scattered fighting still occurring in the southern part of the country, is difficult to discuss or analyze.

To completely comprehend Angola's civil war involves an unraveling of several complex issues: the tribal-ethnic alignments within the liberation movements; the mercenaries; the role of the superpowers—Russia and the United States; and the involvement of Zaire, Zambia, South Africa, and Cuba.

The first sign of trouble occurred shortly after the three liberation movements, MPLA, FNLA, and UNITA, met in 1974 with the outgoing Portuguese administration to form a coalition government. This meeting of the groups, or the Alvor Agreement, was barely six months old when the bickering between MPLA and FNLA developed into a full-scale confrontation.

Many of the problems that existed between the three groups were as ancient as their tribal differences, but it was the more immediate concerns—a dock workers' strike and the control of the economy—that were perhaps most responsible for the bitter fighting that erupted.

In rapid succession, after chasing FNLA and UNITA forces from the capital city of Luanda, MPLA followed with decisive victories along the Angolan coast. With this action, the transitional or coalition government was shattered, and by August 1975 it was officially dissolved. As fighting intensified between MPLA and FNLA, UNITA remained neutral. But before long, an alliance was formed between UNITA and FNLA.

For months the war was virtually a standoff, with each of the movements controlling little more than its traditional tribal land. Then, by late August, South African troops were reported fighting alongside UNITA-FNLA forces. This discovery, and the fact that the United States had also given substantial aid to UNITA and FNLA, critically altered the civil war.

At the beginning of November 1975, with MPLA then reportedly in control of the majority of Angola's provinces, it was decided that additional military aid was needed. In a matter of days, several battalions of combat-ready Cuban troops had joined the ranks of MPLA. The combined firepower of Cuban armor and artillery with Soviet-made rocket launchers quickly turned the tide and by February 1976 UNITA and FNLA had admitted defeat.

Although they had surrendered, each group declared that it would carry on guerilla warfare—FNLA from across the border in Zaire and UNITA from southern Angola. To combat this situation as well as the possibility of South Africa's return, thousands of Cuban troops remain inside Angola.

Dressed in army fatigues and carrying a toy gun and cardboard knife, a young boy marches past a wall covered with political slogans during Angola's recent civil war.

After the Organization of African Unity (OAU) recognized MPLA's People's Government of Angola as the sole legitimate government, the bloody civil war was officially over. The two years of struggle were, in the end, more devastating in their waste of human lives and property than the thirteen-year war against the Portuguese.

ANGOLA TODAY

Although the civil war has officially been concluded and MPLA has gained control of Angola, the troubled economy, political instability, and reconstruction of the country are still monumental problems which have to be dealt with.

In order to profit from the country's rich resources, the nationalization of the economy and the creation of new trade arrangements with the various multinational companies are two things of pressing importance to the leadership of the People's Republic of Angola. Of particular concern is the oil-rich enclave of Cabinda, a strip of land separated from Angola by Zaire, from which more than 200,000 barrels of petroleum a day have been extracted by the Gulf Oil Company.

An earlier attempt by armed guerillas in 1974 was unsuccessful in gaining control of the territory, and the coup was effectively put down by MPLA. Since then, Cabinda (2,895 square miles/7,498 sq km) has been an MPLA resource, and all the Gulf Oil payments have been made to Angola.

Similar agreements have been made with other multinational corporations, but the political and military scene remains in a state of turbulence. The UNITA forces in central Angola, the country's most productive farmland, and its armed struggle along the southern border continues to deter Angola's goal of peace and tranquility. Compounding this problem are the periodic raids by South African militia. Angola's former Defense Minister, Iko Carriera, declared in 1980 that his country was definitely "at war with South Africa."

There have also been problems within Angola's ruling party. Sharp dissension within the ranks has developed into several abortive attempts to overthrow the government. But of all the problems that accompany newly won independence, the death of President Agostinho Neto in September 1979 was perhaps Angola's biggest setback. Replacing such a widely admired and capable leader as Neto will not be easy.

In the days ahead, Angola's People's Republic will surely be tested both from within and from without. That it will meet these challenges in a resolute and forthright manner is as certain as its emergence from under the oppressive heel of Portuguese dominance. "Victory or death," the people cry—and "victory is certain!"

3

MOZAMBIQUE

Mozambique is the second largest of Portugal's ex-colonies. For centuries, because of its midway location on the sea route from Lisbon to India, Mozambique and its coastal region had importance only as a provisioning station for the Portuguese sailors and navigators. Mozambique grew citrus fruits which were used to treat the crews' scurvy—a disease caused by a lack of vitamin C. This remote East African location, as well as the comparatively minor role the territory played in the Atlantic slave trade, are also reasons for so little being known of precolonial Mozambique.

Throughout the colonial period, Mozambique continued to be a mystery for most of the world. But with the emergence of the Front for the Liberation of Mozambique (FRELIMO) and the successful struggle conducted by its freedom fighters, Mozambique has taken its place with the other independent nations of Africa.

LAND, CLIMATE
AND POPULATION

Mozambique's area is 303,075 square miles (784,961 sq km), or roughly twice the size of California. Its 1,737 miles (2,779 km) of coastline run from the country's most northernly point to its southern extremity. All of the principal cities—Pemba, Beira, Xai-Xai, Inhambane, Quelimane, and the capital, Maputo (formerly Lourenço Marques), the largest of the cities, with a population of about 400,000—are situated along the lengthy coastline.

The country is divided into northern and southern sections by the Zambezi river, and is uniquely located between the fertile plains and highlands of south-central Africa and the Indian Ocean. For landlocked countries such as Zambia, Malawi, Zimbabwe, Botswana, and parts of South Africa, the river valleys of Mozambique provide the most accessible land routes to the outside world.

Mozambique's main export commodities are cotton, cane sugar, cashew nuts, copra, tea, and sisal. Subsistence farming barely provides enough food for most of the African population in the country. And the prevalence of the disease-spreading tsetse fly has hindered the development of the cattle industry.

The climate is basically tropical. Each year has both a wet and a dry season. The greatest amount of rainfall occurs during the wet season, lasting from October to April. The wet season also brings higher temperatures. The dry season, from April to September, is cooler than average, with very little rain. A warm ocean current, flowing south from near the equator, raises temperatures and humidity along the coast. Inland, considerable variation occurs in the climate.

The 1976 population of the country was estimated at a little

over nine million, but this figure is generally viewed as inaccurately low. The difficulty of getting to certain regions, the migrations both within Mozambique and between neighboring countries, and disruptions brought on by the struggle for independence are all factors which have hindered an accurate count of the population.

Another important factor in Mozambique's population has been the decrease in the number of Portuguese residents. On the eve of the April 1974 revolution in Portugal, there were 250,000 Portuguese living in Mozambique. By the end of 1976 only 15,000 remained, and many of them had made plans to leave.

ETHNIC GROUPS AND LANGUAGE

To fully understand Mozambican society and ethnic groups, it is necessary to examine and discuss both the traditional and post-independent way of life.

In a traditional manner, the ethnic groups were distributed across three distinct cultural zones. Living north of the Zambezi Valley were people who traced their descent, or ancestry, matrilineally through their mothers' ancestors. In the south, descent was traced patrilineally through the fathers' ancestors. In the Zambezi Valley itself, the lines of descent were mixed. For traditional African society, descent and inheritance play an important role in determining social obligation, religious life, political authority, and economic organization.

*Cattle graze amid coconuts in a
grove of palm trees in Mozambique.*

On the basis of common history, culture, and language, as well as general convenience, the traditional Mozambican population was divided into ten ethnic groupings. The Makua-Lomue of northern Mozambique and the Tsongas to the south were the largest of the ethnic clusters. The lower Zambezi, Shona-Karanga, Islamic coastal, Chopi, Maravi, Yao, Nguni, and the resourceful Makonde comprised the other groups. While little unity existed among these ethnic clusters, there was never any occasion for serious conflict.

Today, in post-independent Mozambique, ethnic and traditional differences are gradually being eradicated. Emphasis is now given to people working together toward the full integration of Mozambican society.

With its aim to minimize ethnic differences, there is also a concern by the present government to improve the network of communication. To this end, Portuguese has been adopted as the official language of the government. In certain sectors of the country, however, Bantu languages such as Ronga and Fanagalo remain the common language. Among the Yao and the Islamic coastal clusters, Arabic and Swahili are widely spoken.

ECONOMY

Before the arrival of Portuguese colonialism, Mozambique's economy was largely limited to farming. This traditional endeavor was often augmented by hunting, and along the coast, fishing. In the early 1960s many of the farmers began to shift from a subsistence economy (where they grew just enough for themselves to eat) to cash crop cultivation and a money economy.

Under colonial rule, Africans were almost completely excluded from both the middle and upper levels of urban economic

*A view of Maputo, Mozambique's capital
and one of Africa's largest ports.*

society. Nor did the kind of economic policies followed during the colonial period allow for much concentration on domestic development.

The economy of Mozambique was directly linked to Portugal. This relationship prevented the establishment of industries that could produce a wide range of products.

Forced labor was another important feature of colonial economics. Later, this practice was extended to include a migrant work force recruited to work in the mines of South Africa and, to a lesser extent, in southern Zimbabwe.

The economy of post-independent Mozambique has objectives and priorities that are very different from the practices of the colonial experience. The country's land and mineral resources now belong entirely to the state, not to Portugal. Private property is rapidly being replaced by collective, socialist ownership. And, agricultural development and education are finally receiving serious attention.

The Constitution of the People's Republic of Mozambique, adopted at the country's independence in 1975, also stated concern for reducing the country's dependence on South Africa, southern Zimbabwe, and Portugal. To date, these plans are being actively pursued, but the crucial lack of financial resources and the shortage of trained and experienced technicians have slowed down the government's plans and the country's progress.

RELIGION, EDUCATION, AND HEALTH

The great majority of Africans in Mozambique still cling to age-old, traditional religious practices. Between 15 to 20 percent of the population are Roman Catholics, and 5 percent are Protestants. There may be 10 percent who are Muslims, chiefly among the Yao of Niassa Province.

The leadership of FRELIMO is explicitly atheist, but according to the Constitution, individuals are guaranteed the freedom to practice or not to practice a religion. This tolerance by FRELIMO of religious practice is seen in the approval given to the United Church of Christ to build a new church in Mozambique.

Before the mass literacy campaigns launched by FRELIMO in recent years, an estimated 85 percent of the population was illiterate. All schools are now state-run and free. Education is closely linked to economic development, and an emphasis is therefore given to reading, vocational training, and student and teacher participation in food production. Political education is also highly promoted. In 1977, more than 16 percent of the nation's budget was spent on education, an expenditure second only to defense.

Like education, medical services and health care under colonialism were virtually nonexistent. Africans who sought medical treatment were forced to travel to the nearest big city. This did not even guarantee service in a population that totaled nine million, with never more than 500 doctors at its peak.

Once FRELIMO assumed full control of the government, medical care improved. Almost immediately, a nationwide vaccination campaign was established to assist the preventive health care programs. And FRELIMO has been recruiting medical doctors from such countries as the People's Republic of China (PRC), the Soviet Union, and Zambia.

Recently, here in the United States, a collective known as the Mozambique Film Project raised nearly 50,000 dollars toward a medical facility for Mozambique. However, Mozambique continues to be in great need of both medical equipment and technicians.

HISTORY

Until more archaeological and anthropological work is done in Mozambique, its beginnings will continue to be vague and uncertain. But there is still enough evidence from the tradition of the Zambezi area to suggest that the country's first inhabitants were related to the Bushmen, or San, a group of hunters and gatherers whose descendants are found in parts of southern Africa.

By the ninth century A.D., Arabs and Arab-influenced African traders were operating along the Mozambican coast. The Arabs formed alliances with African chiefs, and the trade in African ivory, gold, rhinocerous horn, palm oil, and slaves for Arab cloth, glass, beads, and axes brought the Arabs great profits.

In the middle of the fifteenth century, south of Zambezi and stretching to parts of southern Zimbabwe, the great dynasties of the Karanga people arose. Under the leadership of a ruler who came to be known as Mwene Mutapa, the Karanga dominated all the territory between the Zambezi and the Limpopo river, including the rich gold and copper mines.

The Karanga capitals were called *zimbabwe,* and the most famous was Great Zimbabwe, located near present-day Fort Victoria in southern Zimbabwe. Great Zimbabwe was a center of wealth and power, and it is possible today to see remnants of the spectacular stone structures built at that time.

The spread of Mwene Mutapa's empire, and the further

penetration by Muslim merchants and traders into the western interior of Mozambique, resulted in the establishment of huge trading fairs—fairs in which gold was the principal item of exchange. The fairs were profitable to all involved, but especially to the people under Mwene Mutapa who were able to tax all the gold brought to them.

This was the state of affairs in 1487 when a Portuguese scouting expedition, seeking a route to India, landed in Mozambique.

But it was the later visit by Vasco Da Gama in 1498 that would be of greater importance to Portuguese enterprise. Da Gama was amazed by the sophisticated trading society he encountered. Before long, plans were made by the Portuguese to seize control of the ports and strip the Arabs of the lucrative seaborne trade.

The diminishing power of Mwene Mutapa, gradually losing control over his vast empire, gave the Portuguese their opportunity. In the seventeenth century, Mwene Mutapa, to offset the challenge of his African rivals, called on the Portuguese for military assistance. This was a fatal decision that both reduced his prestige and ultimately destroyed what was left of his political authority. By 1629, the Portuguese had gained full control of the Zambezi territories of Mwene Mutapa and his people.

EARLY COLONIALISM
AND AFRICAN RESISTANCE

With the defeat of Mwene Mutapa, Portuguese colonialism was officially launched. Through the manipulations of the *prazeros* (recipients of land leases), the Portuguese crown sought to extend its control beyond the coastal region. However, this plan backfired and the *prazeros* were soon a power independent of the Portuguese crown and acting in defiance of its decrees.

It was not until the 1880s that the power and influence of the *prazeros* was broken. According to a noted historian, the downfall of the *prazeros* was accomplished more by the efforts of the British South African Company than by the Portuguese.

Eventually, with hopes of securing control over Mozambique's interior, the Portuguese crown, copying the British, established a succession of chartered companies. These companies were given almost sovereign power to carry out the business interests of the crown. But this tactic was ineffective and eventually brought more abuse and brutality to the Africans of Mozambique.

If Portugal was still uncertain about its control over the heartland of Mozambique, the problem over external borders was coming to a close. At the meeting of European powers in Berlin in 1884–85, much of the conflict over political boundaries was settled. Portugal's claims in Africa were immediately recognized by France and Germany, but it would be some years later, not until 1891, before Great Britain would recognize Mozambique as Portuguese East Africa.

Throughout this conquest, the Africans resisted when they could. Between 1890 and 1905 there were at least sixteen peasant uprisings in the Zambezi Valley alone. Fortunately for the Portuguese, these revolts were often small and local and had little effect in bringing change or in instilling a higher level of political awareness in the African masses.

The largest of these early rebellions occurred in 1917. When the Portuguese attempted to recruit Africans to fight against the

Germans, the Karanga-Shona group, with their tradition of resistance to colonial rule, began to organize against such forced labor policies. After some initial successes, the Africans were defeated by the superior firepower of the Portuguese. Following the suppression of the revolt, the Portuguese inacted a severe anti-terrorist policy to discourage any further organized rebellions.

Although the Zambezi rebellions failed, they did show that Africans were capable of developing the unity needed to struggle against Portuguese oppression. More than fifty years later, similar uprisings would occur—only this time the outcome would be different.

RISE OF NATIONALISM
AND REVOLUTION

In the 1950s, with the installation of Antonio de Oliveira Salazar's regime in Lisbon, Portugal, the already brutal exploitation of Africans was intensified in Mozambique. Salazar was single-minded in his desire to make Mozambique a successful colony for white Portuguese—even at the expense of African lives.

The rigid system he imposed in Mozambique and throughout Portugal's colonies, or "overseas provinces," had a striking resemblance to the *apartheid* (absolute apartness of blacks and whites) government of South Africa. Segregation, jail, torture, and secret police were some of the means used to keep the Africans in check and to insure Portuguese domination.

As in the past, the Africans again expressed much opposition to these conditions. Dock workers' strikes and protest from Mozambique's elite, educated Africans over poor food supplies and inadequate pay erupted again and again. But not until the militant Mozambicans who had fled to such neighboring coun-

Women made up an important part of FRELIMO's *long fight for independence from Portugal.*

tries as Tanganyika (now Tanzania), Nyasaland (now Malawi), and Northern Rhodesia (now Zambia) returned home, would there truly emerge an effective nationalist movement and a firm strategy for change.

In 1962 three groups—MANU (Mozambique African National Union), UDENAMO (National Democratic Union of Mozambique), and UNAMI (National African Union of Independent Mozambique)—met in a conference at Dar es Salaam, Tanzania, and FRELIMO (Front for the Liberation of Mozambique) was formed. The late Eduardo Chivambu Mondlane, assassinated by Portuguese agents in 1969, was chosen as its first president.

Despite this merger and the creation of a grand council composed of members from all the various organizations, unity was not achieved. The next two years witnessed several splits in the organization. Nevertheless, by 1963, the OAU (Organization of African Unity) and its Liberation Committee had granted full status to FRELIMO as the only Mozambican liberation movement.

As the military campaigns inside Mozambique increased, FRELIMO was also busy winning support from foreign sources. The Communist states in Europe and Asia provided both military equipment and financial aid; diplomatic support came from the United Nations; and, perhaps most importantly, neighboring Tanzania offered the liberation movement aid—refugee camps, a political headquarters, military training, and educational opportunities.

To halt the advancing struggle, the Portuguese resorted to several defensive measures. One of the more significant tactics was the creation of *aldeamentos,* or centralized artificial villages, where the Portuguese sought to cut off contact between FRELIMO and the African villages.

In the other Portuguese colonies, particularly Angola and Guinea-Bissau, the struggle for independence was in motion and the Portuguese were now forced to fight on three vital fronts. Gradually, resentment toward Portugal's policies in the colonies was stirring the masses in Lisbon and throughout Portugal. Finally, in 1974, a group of military officers seized power in Portugal and announced that one of their major objectives would be to end the wars in the colonies.

After centuries of colonial rule and ruthless abuse from the chartered companies, FRELIMO and a decade of guerilla warfare brought an end to Portuguese domination in Mozambique. On June 25, 1975 Mozambique became the second of Portugal's colonies to win its independence.

MOZAMBIQUE TODAY

Now that Mozambique has gained its independence, there is still much to be done. *A Luta Continua!* (The Struggle Continues!) is a phrase that is heard often among the people of Mozambique. They are determined to reconstruct their society, a society which suffered under many years of Portuguese colonialism.

Under the guidance of FRELIMO, most of the basic human needs—health care, food, clothing, housing, and education—are now available to all Mozambicans, regardless of race or class. At the same time, the government is working hard to eliminate poverty, prostitution, disease, illiteracy, and infant mortality.

To combat the divisiveness of colonialism, the government is also moving to create for Mozambique a common national identity. Racism, tribalism, and sexism, widespread during colonial rule, are slowly being eradicated. Where women are concerned, the president of Mozambique, Samora Machel, has noted

*Thousands of people fled the recent war
for independence in nearby Zimbabwe and sought
safety in refugee camps in Mozambique.*

that "the participation of Mozambican women in all sectors [of the society] is an essential condition for the triumph of our revolution."

Although Mozambique has a communist rather than capitalist ideology, it is nonetheless free of Soviet and Chinese influence. In fact, it is developing its own unique socialist economic structure and considers itself among the non-aligned nations of the world. To date, the U.S. government has not given any significant aid to Mozambique.

This lack of economic assistance is of pressing importance to Mozambique, which, according to the International Red Cross, is still sheltering thousands of refugees from the recent struggle for independence in nearby Zimbabwe (formerly known as Rhodesia).

All of these burdens weigh heavily on the country's economy, struggling to free itself from dependency on neighboring South Africa. Revenues from South Africa's use of its railway system and its port of Maputo are important contributions to Mozambique's economy. Even the magnificent Cabora Bassa Dam primarily supplies power for South Africa, and this has delayed FRELIMO's plans for electrification of Mozambique's countryside.

Mozambique has been a sovereign and independent nation for only five years, and although great improvements have been made, there remain many obstacles to hurdle. But the Mozambican people are determined, and they face the future with the same strength and fortitude that broke the shackles of colonialism. They, above all, know that it will not be easy. *A Luta Continua!*

4

GUINEA-BISSAU AND THE CAPE VERDE ISLANDS

Guinea-Bissau (formerly Portuguese Guinea) and the Cape Verde Islands, were the first of the ex-colonies to be explored by the Portuguese. Having neither Angola's mineral wealth nor Mozambique's strategic location, Guinea-Bissau and Cape Verde were of the least importance to Portugal.

Also, unlike Angola or Mozambique, the smaller Guinea-Bissau never experienced settlements of Europeans. The Cape Verde Islands, more than 350 miles (563 km) into the Atlantic Ocean, were uninhabited before the Portuguese came. The population of the islands gradually increased as African slaves, mainly from Guinea-Bissau, were captured and brought to work there on plantations.

Guinea-Bissau and Cape Verde are often discussed together but there is actually a separate history for each country. During the period of armed struggle against the Portuguese launched in 1963, an attempt was made by the leadership of the

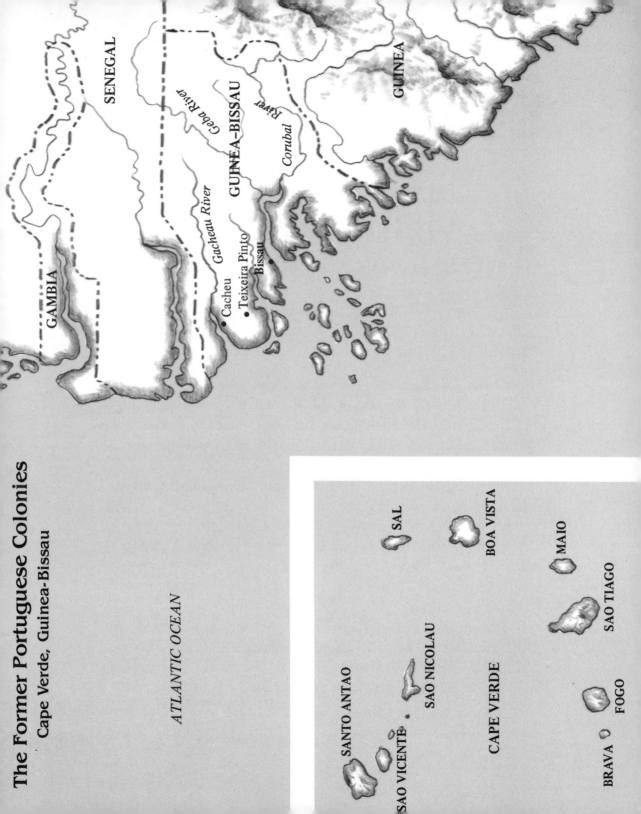

The Former Portuguese Colonies
Cape Verde, Guinea-Bissau

GAMBIA

SENEGAL

GUINEA-BISSAU

GUINEA

Geba River

Gacheau River

Corubal River

Cacheu

Teixeira Pinto

Bissau

ATLANTIC OCEAN

CAPE VERDE

SANTO ANTAO

SAO VICENTE

SAO NICOLAU

SAL

BOA VISTA

MAIO

SAO TIAGO

FOGO

BRAVA

various liberation movements to combine their political and military goals. The formation in 1956 of the African Party for the Liberation of Guinea and the Cape Verde Islands (PAIGC) is indicative of this desire for unity.

Under the direction of PAIGC, the revolutionaries of Guinea-Bissau and Cape Verde were instrumental in helping Guinea-Bissau achieve its independence almost a year before Angola and Mozambique.

GUINEA-BISSAU:
GEOGRAPHY, CLIMATE,
AND POPULATION

Guinea-Bissau was known at one time as Portuguese Guinea to distinguish it from the neighboring Republic of Guinea. Surrounded by Senegal and Guinea, Guinea-Bissau is a relatively flat country whose map shape and area of 13,948 square miles (36,125 sq km) resembles a hand with short fingers reaching out to its islands in the sea.

The general terrain of Guinea-Bissau is composed of low tablelands to the northeast, a dense forest zone at the center, and a coastal plain to the south. The nearly tropical climate, has, in fact, two seasons: a rainy season from June to September and a dry season for the rest of the year.

With much of its territory in the lowlands, including the nearby Bijagoes Archipelago, Guinea-Bissau is periodically flooded with tidal waters. At the base of the narrow estuaries, or between the "fingers" of Guinea-Bissau, are the rivers upon which are located the chief ports of Cacheu, Teixeira Pinto, and the largest city, Bissau.

The population of Guinea-Bissau has been estimated at above 800,000 (before the war with Portugal), which gives the country a density of almost sixty people per square mile, an unusually high percentage for tropical Africa. The majority of these people, scattered among thirty or more tribes, live along the riverbanks.

The major ethnic groups are the Balantes (250,000), the Manjaks (140,000), the Fulas (100,000), and the Mandingoes (80,000). The numerous Balantes would eventually figure prominently in the resistance and the revolution against the Portuguese. Other important groups are the Pepels, the Felupes, the Bissagos, and the Mancags or Brames.

ECONOMY, EDUCATION, AND SOCIAL STRUCTURE

Before the invasion of the Portuguese, most people eked out a meagre living by farming. Later, these same African-owned farms would be the source from which the Portuguese would derive their wealth.

Traditionally, groundnuts (peanuts) have been the mainstay of agricultural production. But in the twentieth century, with the arrival of the mestiços from Cape Verde, rice became the main crop and the country's basic food. Palm kernels, wood, coconuts, sugarcane, and vegetable oils are also products of some importance to the economy. Because of the lack of electrical power and transportation facilities, industrial development has never been of any real significance.

Unlike Angola and Mozambique, there were no great multinational corporations in Guinea-Bissau. In this context, the

*Once a vital force in Guinea-Bissau's
fight for independence, the women of
Guinea-Bissau will now work alongside
the men for improvements in their country's
economy, education, and health care.*

country more accurately reflected a true colonial appendage of Portugal.

As in the other colonies, education for the Africans in Guinea-Bissau was left almost entirely to the Catholic missionaries, who, despite their dedication, were basically ineffective in relieving the high rate of illiteracy. Spread over the country were also some five hundred Muslim elementary schools, but since they put greater emphasis on teaching religion than on academics, they brought little change to this critical situation.

The social structure before the revolution was characterized by the division between Animists, or those who followed traditional African beliefs, attributing spirit life to inanimate things, and Muslims, those who under Arab influence, converted to the religion of Islam, and between urban and rural dwellers. The Animists represented more than 70 percent of the population and were comprised mostly of Balantes.

Muslims were represented by the Fulas and the Mandingoes. The greatest number of traveling merchants and traders were recruited from these two ethnic groups. These two groups, particularly their families of nobility, were among the first Africans to go over to the Portuguese side during the war.

Generally, the Animist peasants and the rural lower middle class were receptive to the call of revolution. In the urban centers, only the wage laborers responded as a matter of course to the developing struggle. Practically all of the other classes, including the unemployed drifters, were reluctant to join the liberation movements. The city youth, however, possessing a certain amount of education, played an important role in the urban struggle, and many of them were counted among the middle rank of the PAIGC.

HISTORICAL PERSPECTIVE:
RESISTANCE AND REVOLUTION

In the middle 1400s, Portugal's early venture in Guinea-Bissau was a direct result of the country's desire to control trade in west Africa and to find Christian allies to assist them in overcoming Islam. To accomplish this task, it was necessary to build strategically located forts that would also assist them in the movement and in the storage of slaves.

Except for occasional triumphs by the Dutch and Muslim forces, the Portuguese were uncontested in the control of the slave trade. However, after the slave trade was brought to a close in the nineteenth century, the Portuguese lost interest in Guinea-Bissau and the territory was almost seized by the French. From this point on, the history of Guinea-Bissau is not unlike the history that unfolded in the other colonies during the same period—endless conflict over control of the land between the indigenous Africans and the Portuguese.

By the dawn of the twentieth century this combat had greatly intensified, and for the next forty years there were claims from the Portuguese that the country was theirs and completely pacified. The falsity of such claims became evident in the 1950s when the many sporting clubs, like the cultural associations in Angola at the same time, became beehives of political activity.

The creation of the Movement for the National Independence of Portuguese Guinea (MING) by intellectuals from Cape Verde and Guinea-Bissau was an immediate outgrowth of intolerable work and social conditions. In the realm of health care, the Portuguese had done nothing to stem the spread of such tropical diseases as malaria, hookworms, and sleeping sickness, which afflicted half the population in Guinea-Bissau. Infant mortality stood at an astounding 600 per thousand and there was only one doctor for every 100,000 people.

Two years later, in 1956, MING had evolved into PAIGC and the move toward armed struggle was accelerated. The PAIGC was closely aligned with MPLA in Angola and FRELIMO in Mozambique. One of the key members of PAIGC, Amilcar Cabral, would later be the first Secretary-General of the party.

The wave of strikes that occurred in 1958 was ignited by the members of PAIGC. A year later, the dock workers' strike at Pidgiguiti (in which fifty workers were killed), prompted the PAIGC to revise its strategy and plan of action.

With Cabral assuming control of the party at this juncture, plans for war were prepared and, shortly thereafter, the PAIGC established headquarters outside the country in the Republic of Guinea. In the following years, the struggle continued in the towns and in the countryside, with the party expanding its organizing efforts. By the winter of 1963, the first stage of armed struggle was launched as small bands of PAIGC troops began to slip across the border from the Republic of Guinea into Guinea-Bissau.

The pattern of guerilla warfare conducted so successfully in Angola and Mozambique was also carried out in Guinea-Bissau. And like the other colonies, when the Portuguese officers revolted in 1974, PAIGC's situation was vastly improved. Slowly, the long fight against the Portuguese was grinding to a halt. The end finally came in August, 1974, when agreement was reached on the terms of independence for Guinea-Bissau.

Unfortunately, like his counterpart in Mozambique, Eduardo Mondlane, the great leader of PAIGC, Amilcar Cabral did not live to see the flag of independence fly over his country.

On January 20, 1973 Cabral was assassinated in Conakry, Guinea, by Portuguese agents.

GUINEA-BISSAU TODAY

It has been over five years since independence was won in Guinea-Bissau, and the job of rebuilding a war-torn society continues to be a primary task. The problem of resettling refugees, clearing away the explosive mines from rural roads, and restoring the economy were some of the immediate challenges that faced the new government.

Guinea-Bissau, once self-sufficient in its crops of rice, in recent years has had to import tons of it annually. There is still no mining industry, and in the manufacturing sector there are fewer than two thousand workers. On the other hand, the growth of the newly developed export-oriented fishing industry brightens an otherwise gloomy economic picture.

Problems also exist in the realm of unification. On a smaller scale, there is the potential danger that comes from the demobilized African soldiers, mainly Fulas, who fought for the Portuguese. But according to the government, there is no real trouble between the PAIGC and the Fulas, and compared to most countries in Africa, Guinea-Bissau is today peaceful and stable.

On a much larger scale is the issue of unity with the Cape Verde Islands. Over the last few years, relations between the two countries have shown great improvement. They already share a judicial system and a maritime transport company. A joint airline is now under study.

Although the PAIGC has been struggling rigorously to remain independent of the major world powers, trade relations with the West are increasing daily. And, quite ironically for a

[45]

country that waged a revolution with arms from the Soviet Union and China, much of this trade and aid is coming from some of the most conservative capitalist governments in the world.

Guinea-Bissau has come a long way down the road of independence, and under the guidance of PAIGC they are sure to go much further. The leadership of the country, including the able president, Luis Cabral, is realistic and pragmatic about the days ahead, and in the spirit of their well-remembered patriot, Amilcar Cabral, they appear to be "telling no lies and claiming no easy victories."

CAPE VERDE:
GEOGRAPHY, ECONOMY
AND POPULATION

The crescent-shaped Cape Verde Islands, despite their 375 miles (604 km) from the African mainland, have been historically paired with Guinea-Bissau. The traditional link between the two countries is well-grounded, although they were officially separated administratively in 1879.

When the Portuguese began to move along the coastline of West Africa in the mid-1400s, Cape Verde was uninhabited. Two hundred years later, these islands of volcanic origin were thickly populated with Africans brought to farm the numerous Portuguese plantations.

Carrying their country's flag and wearing shirts picturing Amilcar Cabral, young people of Guinea-Bissau marched shortly after independence was declared in 1974.

Cape Verde consists of ten rather mountainous islands and five islets with a total area of over 1,557 square miles (3,567 sq km). There are few natural resources available on the islands, and even subsistence farming, so common elsewhere in Africa, is uncertain here because of the frequent droughts. Some of the islands do contain large salt deposits, and some of this is sold to other African countries.

The islands chief economic importance is as a refueling station for ships and aircraft. The main occupation of the 300,000 people is fishing and breeding of livestock.

Cape Verde's population is basically a mixture of Africans, exiled Portuguese convicts, and Jews expelled from Portugal during the Spanish Inquisition (1492–1769). With more than 60 percent of its people with mixed ancestry, Cape Verde is very atypical of Portugal's African colonies.

The uncommon percentage of mestiços also accounts for the unique semblance of racial integration and assimilation that occurred in Cape Verde. Their strong identification with Portugal was reinforced in 1950 when all residents of Cape Verde were declared full citizens of Portugal.

RESISTANCE AND LINKS
TO GUINEA-BISSAU

If some mestiços felt they belonged to Portuguese society, there were others who did not suffer such delusions. This was espe-

Cape Verde consists of ten mountainous islands and five smaller islets.

cially true for those Cape Verdeans who managed to obtain a university education and had opportunities to associate with other African students.

From the ranks of these graduates and intellectuals came the radicals who would become the key organizers of resistance and revolution in the Portuguese colonies. The late Amilcar Cabral, Henri Labery, and Luis Cabral, now the president of Guinea-Bissau, are a few of the noteworthy Cape Verdeans who greatly influenced the successful liberation movement.

The relationship between the people of Cape Verde and Guinea-Bissau is perhaps best illustrated by the name of the organization that led the revolutionary struggle—the African Party for the Independence of Guinea and Cape Verde (PAIGC). Although there were moments of disagreement over the heavy emphasis on matters pertaining exclusively to Guinea-Bissau or the prominent role of Cape Verdeans in the leadership of PAIGC, on the whole, the bond between the two countries and their people was strengthened.

The movement of Cape Verdeans to Guinea-Bissau has been a notable factor over the years. Guinea-Bissau owes its development of rice to the incoming Cape Verdeans as well as the Cape Verdean Creole that is widely spoken in both countries. By 1970, there were 3,500 mestiços from Cape Verde in Guinea-Bissau.

Schoolboys gather outside
their classroom at an
elementary school on Cape Verde.

The two countries' contact extends beyond ethnic origin, culture, and language. Attempts are now being made to unify the people along economic and political lines as well.

The dependency of Guinea-Bissau on Cape Verde disappeared many years ago and, to some degree, has been reversed today. The severe drought which devastated the Sahel has also reached Cape Verde, leaving the country with little or nothing to export. The exchange of cement for wood from Guinea-Bissau appears to be the only optimistic sign on Cape Verde's economic horizon.

At one time, Cape Verde's economy was bolstered by income from emigrants who had settled in the United States, particularly in Massachusetts, Rhode Island, and parts of California. But the restrictions placed on emigration gradually began to limit the amount of money these people could send from abroad.

5

THE OTHER ISLANDS: SÃO TOMÉ AND PRÍNCIPE

The islands of São Tomé and Príncipe are the smallest of Portugal's ex-colonies in Africa. These two islands of only 372 square miles (964 sq km) have a history that is quite similar to Cape Verde's.

About 125 miles (201 km) off the coast of Africa, in the Gulf of Guinea and some 80 miles (129 km) apart, São Tomé and Príncipe were first explored by the Portuguese in 1471, and for many years the islands were used for holding the African slaves prior to their shipment to the West. Its population of 69,000 began with a collection of Portuguese convicts, Jews, and African slaves.

The principal industry is commercial agriculture, and copra (the kernel of coconut), palm oil, and bananas are the leading export items. The temperature, which ranges between 66° F (19° C) and 89° F (32° C), also makes the climate ideally

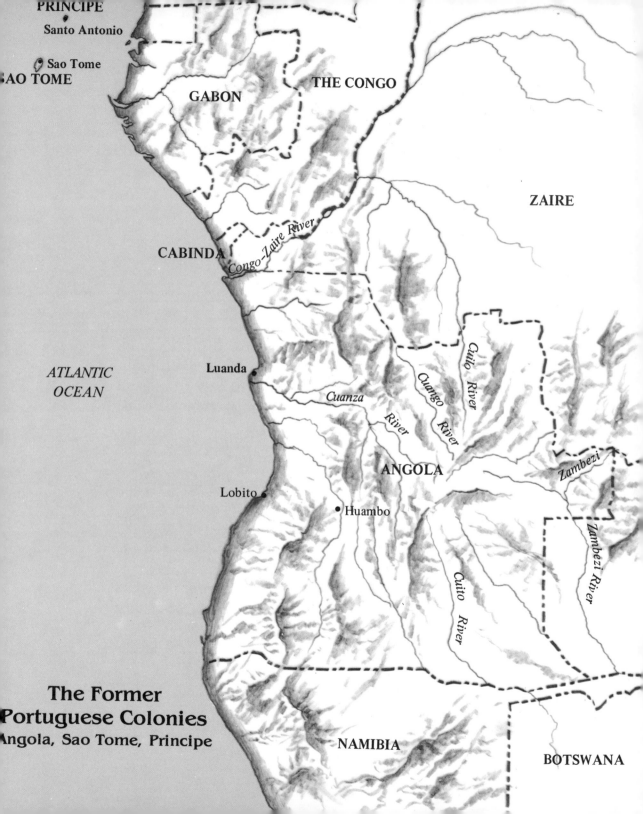

PRINCIPE
Santo Antonio

Sao Tome
SAO TOME

GABON

THE CONGO

ZAIRE

CABINDA

Congo-Zaire River

ATLANTIC
OCEAN

Luanda

Cuanza

River

Cuango River

Cuito River

Zambezi

ANGOLA

Lobito

Huambo

Cuito River

Zambezi River

The Former
Portuguese Colonies
Angola, Sao Tome, Principe

NAMIBIA

BOTSWANA

suited for the cultivation of sugarcane and coffee. Both São Tomé and Príncipe are volcanic islands with jagged mountains out of which large plantations have been carved. The plantations, of course, were all owned by the Portuguese.

When the Portuguese colonies experienced the wave of nationalism elsewhere in the 1950s, São Tomé and Príncipe were not excluded. In 1953, on São Tomé, Portuguese police massacred a thousand native Africans who were protesting the intolerable labor conditions. This incident was the catalyst for widespread resistance throughout the islands.

At the beginning of the sixties, the island students at Portuguese universities extended the struggle through the creation of the Liberation Committee of São Tomé and Príncipe. Out of this organization the Movement for the Liberation of São Tomé and Príncipe evolved and would eventually carry the bulk of the successful struggle for independence.

In July 1975, the long-sought freedom from Portugal was gained, and Manuel Pinto Da Costa, the leader of the movement, became the nation's first president.

Since independence, life on São Tomé and Príncipe has generally improved, but there remain severe economic problems. Most of these problems facing the two islands stem from the continuing reliance on cocoa, which has suffered from record-low world prices on the export market.

To remedy this situation and to stimulate the sagging economies, meetings have been held between island officials and business representatives from the United States. Renewed trade agreements with Portugal should also bring some additional revenue.

FOR FURTHER READING

Addison, John. *Ancient Africa*. New York: John Day, 1970.

The Encyclopedia of Africa. New York: Franklin Watts, 1976.

Murphy, E. Jefferson. *Understanding Africa*. New York: Thomas Y. Crowell, 1978.

Page, J. D. *A History of Africa*. New York: Knopf, 1978.

INDEX